Faith Journey

God's Divine Interruptions

Pursuing God's Purposes and Destiny

Woodrow F. Blok

Harvest Leadership Publishing

Faith Journey: God's Divine Interruptions

Attn: Dr. Woodrow F. Blok
P.O. Box 765176
Dallas, Texas 75376
woodynmel@gmail.com
goodnews4asia@gmail.com

Readers should be aware that any Internet addresses (websites, blogs, etc.) offered as citations and/or resources for further information may have changed or disappeared between the time this was written and when it is read. They are only offered as a resource, and not endorsed. All Scriptures are quoted from the New King James Version, unless otherwise noted.

Limit of Liability/Disclaimer of Warranty: The author, editor and publisher have used their best efforts in preparing this book; however, no representations or warranties with respect to the accuracy or completeness of the contents of this book and specifically disclaim any implied warranties of merchantability or fitness for a particular purpose. No warranty may be created or extended by sales representatives or written sales materials
peru

Table of Contents

Dedication

I gratefully dedicate this book to my family who has stood by my side over the years. My beloved wife, Melanie and daughter, Shini, have encouraged me throughout my journey.

Secondly, I dedicate this book to pastors, leaders and members of Overcomers Church, Oasis Fellowship and the KMK Prayer Network in Sri Lanka. All have played an incredible role and been a part of this very exciting, transformational journey together.

Finally, amazing spiritual fathers, mothers, mentors, and many other excellent servants of God who were used to touch and impact my life over the years.

The vision that was given to me by God would not have happened without our faithful donors and supporters who believed in our vision and were there when we needed them.

Above all, I dedicate this book to the Lord Jesus Christ. We give you praise and honor and glory for the good things you are doing around the globe.

Introduction

God's Divine Interruptions were actually God's profound opportunities!

As I have traveled my faith journey, I realize that God's Divine Interruptions redirected my journey in many ways. All of them good! But also, it caused me to transform my approach to ministry. When I started my Christian expedition, my dreams were only the starting point. My dreams were expanded and "rocked" my world. I could have never dreamed how exciting my journey would be.

Currently, I realize I have many more years to go, so I think, *God, what are you going to do in the next 25 to 30 years?* I know God's Divine Interruptions are going to be fantastic.

In my faith journey God didn't show me all the challenges. He didn't show me how I would overcome all the obstacles and hindrances. God is wise! I probably would have *backed out.*

I am sharing my life's story with the hope that it will help and inspire many to pursue their God-given dreams, their true purpose and destiny. No matter what the challenges, pitfalls, trials, and tribulations you may encounter, you are able to overcome them all, for with God all things are possible. My story is about practical spirituality in action. It is inspirational but also true facts.

I am thankful for my loving wife, Melanie, even in the midst of the insurmountable situations, she somehow knew how to trust God, and believed in my ability to hear from God.

Besides learning many valuable and important lessons, I learned to hear God's voice. I learned to develop mountain moving faith, faced and overcame life-threatening persecutions, and saw God perform marvelous miracles of healing, deliverance, signs and wonders, and much more. It's been amazing to see how God chose someone who began with zero ministry finances and changed it to a nonprofit organization with $1,000,000+ in assets and an operation with 25 full-time employees. This is major as the annual GDP is $3,818.[1] God has provided this without a major ministry organization or denomination support or a significant amount of monthly support. Every day Melanie and I and our leaders must hear the voice of God and trust him to provide for our needs, including Shepherds Heart Childrens Home, a family-style home for 16 girls.

I pray that you will learn some of the secrets of going forward or that it will be a reinforcement of what you already know for your own success on your faith journey.

Melanie and I are very grateful to those who have partnered by providing finances, prayer, encouragement and support in order to be a part of God's vision in our lives.

---

[1] https://en.wikipedia.org/wiki/Economy_of_Sri_Lanka

Chapter 1

Hearing the Call

I have made you a light for the Gentiles,
that you may bring salvation to the ends
of the earth.

Acts 13:47

On April 8, 1988, I arrived in Dallas, Texas. For a person like me who had lived in Colombo, Sri Lanka, it was a total culture shock to say the least. The nation was in tremendous turmoil, and the unstable economy was shifting slowly from primarily agricultural to industrial. The future was dismal because of the civil strife.

The trip to the United States was an award for our marketing and sales achievements. The Ricoh Company in Japan recognized our efforts by granting us a $3,000, all-expenses paid trip from Sri Lanka to the West Coast of the U.S.A. A colleague and I joined about 40 other top sales people from many Asian countries.

Our tour included San Francisco, Los Angeles and Las Vegas. We flew in planes, traveled in luxury coaches, enjoyed dinners at fine dining restaurants and received royal treatment for six days. Within six days the tour ended. For a young Asian man, the bubble of the dream life ended too quickly!

Nervously I managed to locate and board a Greyhound coach in Los Angeles, after saying good-bye to the group. I traveled by Greyhound bus for 36 hours, and I arrived in Dallas to stay with a friend for a few months. I wanted to stay in America as long as I could without breaking the visa requirements.

During the first month, I met many people, mostly from the Texas area but also some from other states and nations. I enjoyed meeting several young people from Christ For The Nations Institute (CFNI), which was about five minutes away from where I was staying. This was the first time I heard about the Bible school even though it had a reputation internationally. The school had a worldwide reach to nations globally. The school had Bible and leadership courses and meetings that were open to the public.

The first time I attended a service at CFNI, I was impacted significantly. The main institute building was full and the lights were low. The song, "Think About His Love" was playing. It was like a glimpse of Heaven. I thought, *I have never been in a church with a setting like this.* As a musician who had played in churches in Sri Lanka as well as other places, I liked the music and was greatly amazed.

While staying with my friend, students from CFNI who I had met seemed assertive saying things like, "You look like someone who needs to attend CFNI." I always politely declined, "The idea sounds good, but that isn't really for me." They were all very excited and passionate which irritated my religious feathers that were greatly ruffled at their comments.

Divine interruption
Within a few weeks, however, I started to sense God was speaking to me about attending CFNI. Long after the jetlag stopped affecting me, I would lie awake at night pondering my next step in life in the U.S.A. A Scripture repeatedly kept coming to me, especially the phrase, "Do not exalt yourself, in the king's presence and do not claim a place among great men; it is better for him to say come up here" (Proverbs 25:6). It was like a resounding echo in my head. Earlier I had retorted to the echo by saying, "CFNI does not give students an accredited bachelor's degree!" I wanted a transcript to carry on to the next place of higher education. My head was about earning a transcript, not at all about a life transformation.

After four months of resisting, I decided to say to God, "OK, I will attend for a semester, and you will see how unfit I am for this Bible school." I thought to myself, *God will surely get tired of trying to keep me in Bible school. And He would let me go pursue a business degree or whatever degree I desired.*

Many students for underdeveloped Third World Nations usually attend with a work scholarship. They go

13

to school in the morning and after lunch work on the CFNI campus. I did not have such a scholarship. When I enrolled and started attending classes, I had just enough money for one semester. Because I had received a student visa and was a nonimmigrant, I could not work a regular job and earn income. I had no sponsoring church, and no pledges from any people or organizations. So, kicking and screaming I started one week late with just enough faith to dare to embark on a faith journey I had never walked on previously.

Chapter 2

Secret Weapon: Prayer

The effectual fervent prayer of a righteous
man is powerful and affective.

James 5:16

When we think of giving ourselves to receive training at
a Bible school, we don't have much doubt that prayer is
a very important spiritual discipline to cultivate.
Attending a world-renowned Bible school known for
spiritual warfare may give us the idea that prayer and
intercession would come naturally. It wasn't so! Many
wonderful activities like high quality praise and worship,
excellent, anointed teachers, instructors and classes
along with an international student body is the perfect
setting for spiritual growth. But the discipline of personal
prayer was not easy to cultivate.

I am very, very thankful that God connected me
with a prayer intercessor a couple of weeks into the first

semester. This man invited me to pray with him two to three times a week. I was quite excited to join. The only problem I encountered was he wasn't short winded. The prayer times would go on for two to three hours. Although it was very good, I didn't want to put so much time into prayer. After a couple of times, I would hide myself and not answer the door when my prayer partner came to my room looking for me. I would pretend I was not in my room, and he would leave. When we would meet again, I offered him excuses for not being there. However, he persevered and kept after me. After a month or two, I started to enjoy or value those prayer times more and more.

The prayer room and library chapel became the most sought-after place for us. I am thankful to God and my friend. I learned to hear God's voice, develop sensitivity to the Holy Spirit, patiently wait in His presence and praying through for needs and situations. We warred together against spiritual enemies and much, much more. Sometimes I was still and silent for hours in His presence. Many quality prayer times took place. Some were personal, some with the two of us together and other times with a group of several students and even instructors joining in. Those times were powerful, creative, prophetic, exciting, anointed, revelatory, and refreshing.

I remember a specific time when I was by myself in the balcony at the Institute Building. This was the sanctuary where the primary services and chapels were held. The presence of God was extremely strong. The presence was so powerful after about four hours, I

16

absolutely did not want to leave, even though it was time to go to the cafeteria for dinner, served from five to six pm. But I just did not want to leave His wonderful presence! Food and drink, mingling with excited people were bargain-basement prices, and it lost its important when Holy Spirit showed up. Anyone who entered into the manifest presence wanted to bask in His glory. Just like basking in the sun on a beautiful beach, I wanted to enjoy Him as long as I possibly could. Holy Spirit was cleansing, healing, and delivering. He was breaking me and shaping me so I would become an entirely new and transformed person. He was preparing me to partner with Him for the future. I was learning to set my agenda aside time and time again to choose what He wanted. Even as I drove the CFN security truck around the 80+ acre campus doing my job, day after day, I would pray in tongues for hours and hours. This was what I wanted to experience, His manifest presence, refreshing and empowering me constantly. I prayed in the spirit about everything I would encounter when I returned to my nation, because I knew it was not going to be easy.

I am so thankful and grateful because if I had not learned to use this secret weapon effectively, I am confident that the outcome would be much different. If I did not know how to get a hold of God in the CFNI spiritual bubble, it would have been incredibly difficult, tragic and dangerous. I was called to pioneer and build by serving in a spiritual graveyard. When I returned to my nation, Sri Lanka, I experienced all types of persecution from radically hostile Buddhists, Hindus and Muslims when pioneering churches and ministries. The secret weapon of prayer was the only one thing that gave me the strength to prevail.

Throughout the years, I have observed students who did not take advantage of the opportunities while in the CFNI spiritual bubble. Some strayed away, gave up on the call or did not rise up and pursue their God-given destiny. Every time the arrow pointed toward one major factor to prayerlessness and lack of hunger for His presence. There were other factors as well, but this was one of the major reasons.

The CFNI spiritual bubble is the open heaven and the heavenly space that the ministry has labored hard to establish and advance for multiple generations. Our goal should be to take the anointing and the authority to establish our own spiritual open heaven, our heavenly space, where God assigns for us.

> You shall see heaven open and the angels of God ascending and descending.
>
> John 1:51

Chapter 3

Giving and Receiving

Give and it shall be given unto you.

Luke 6:38

The offering buckets were passed row by row at the Tuesday night service at CFNI. Students and visitors alike knew that this was a standard for every service on Tuesday nights and Sunday afternoons. In my student days I did not have even enough money to give a few dollars in the offering. Everything I was earning was designated to pay for my Bible school bill which included tuition, housing and food. After working for five months, 20 hours weekly, washing dishes in the cafeteria and working security, the income covered only 30% of my school bill for each semester. Looking at it from the beginning, it was a losing proposition. Every semester I would have to exercise my spiritual faith and believe that God would miraculously supply the 70% balance.

Never in my life of 24 years had I taken such a huge risk. However, God gave me a lasting peace and deep assurance that He would somehow supply.

Put all you have in the offering bucket

On one particular night when the offering bucket was coming closer to me, I heard a whisper, *Take everything that you have in your wallet and give it to the plastic bucket.* I only had about $40 and that was designated for the school bill. I was in absolute shock! In fact, I thought it was the enemy so I began to whisper softly, *I rebuke you, Satan! I know what you want to do. You are trying to make me an absolute pauper.* I watched the bucket pass me by and ignored the voice. I settled down to listen to the speaker. However, I couldn't concentrate for the rest of the evening.

Later that night I tried to sleep but was wide awake. No sleep! No peace! And a deep sense of having grieved Holy Spirit was what I was experiencing. After a sleepless night, in the morning I was sleepy. I was exhausted! With absolutely no peace, I looked for the head usher and found him so I could put my very, very precious money in his hand. My $40 was in an envelope! I asked the man, "Please, put this in last night's offering. This has caused me a sleepless night." Smiling, he consoled me and moved on. Immediately, I experienced an incredible peace so sweet that it filled my heart. The peace that passes all understanding was guarding my heart. I learned a valuable lesson. When my peace was taken away, I needed to stop and listen to what Holy Spirit was trying to say. He was trying to get my attention to learn a series of precious lessons that impacted me for the rest of my life. God was teaching me to follow His leading. He wanted me to totally depend upon Him with full, immediate obedience. This lesson prepared me for the many, many financial mountains I would be facing in the future.

A few months later I started to notice supernatural mini-miracles were taking place. Someone anonymously paid for voice lessons. Another brought food to me when I had a very hungry stomach as I was working at the security base office. He said, "God was prompting me to bring this food to you. Do you think you may need it?" Need it? "Yes, yes, very much!" I thanked the man and gobbled the food before he could leave the room. Little by little miraculously my needs were being met. My heart was beating with excitement.

By late September 1989, in the middle of the fourth semester; however, all my efforts to pay my school bill were proving futile. The debt had continued to pile up, and it seemed huge to me. I desperately wanted to continue my studies and graduate with my class the following year. The finance office continued to be overly gracious to me and allowed me to make payments, no matter how small the amount. One day I received a note from the finance office. They wanted me to see the registrar. I was trembling as I went. I thought, *I am done. This is the end. I will be dismissed from school. I will have to return to Sri Lanka and would not be fully prepared for the ministry that I dreamed about.* It was a very long 400 yards to the registrar's office. I walked with a heavy heart from the cafeteria at the Gordon

Lindsay Tower to the Student Center. My faithful prayer partner accompanied me and tried to encourage me but with very little success. When I reached the registrar's office, I was totally taken by surprise. Dr. Belcher, Director of International Student Affairs, informed me that I had received a Gordon Lindsay scholarship. This was a special fund, and I was one of three recipients. Because of my persistence and perseverance, they believed I was worthy to receive this donation. The scholarship paid up all the arrears and even through graduation. Occasionally, I had heard about others receiving sudden surprises; miraculous, anonymous school bill payments. But this was my first real experience! Instantly, I felt incredible joy and relief. I felt like I was floating on air.

Then the larger miracles were starting to happen! Friends would give me $100 or $200. Surprisingly, my little home church in Sri Lanka gave $500 to help with completing my training. I was tremendously grateful to receive all the donations. I learned another valuable lesson. We don't fulfill our assignments by ourselves. Many, many others contribute to make our journey possible and successful. I am thankful for all who have become part of my journey. I am grateful for each person who obeyed the inner voice in them to donate for the purpose of advancing the Kingdom of God.

It is also important for us to recognize and honor the people who have donated. My very good friend, Kit Mudalige who lives in Kandy, Sri Lanka, was a great source of encouragement and strength. Many people have helped and sacrificed. It is a team effort, and we should not forget those who have believed in us.

Not every opportunity is from God.

When it was approaching the time to return to Sri Lanka to follow the vision and leading of the Lord, my spirit was wanting to stay in the U.S. It was a war-ravaged nation. One war in the North, and another in the South. At that time the nation was one of the top countries in the world for terrorism. In addition, it was one of the top nations for persecution. Living and ministering in Sri Lanka would involve taking serious risks and making great sacrifices.

My training ended, and I knew my visa would end so I really did not have a choice but to return to my nation, Sri Lanka, in October 1990.

God's interruption! Return to Sri Lanka!

I reserved my airline ticket to return. The travel agent, a man originally from the nation of India, asked, "Why are you going back to Sri Lanka? It is facing so much war, just stay! I will give you a ticketing job and help you obtain your green card, permanent residency status. It was so very appealing for a young man like me who had no resources and would soon lose his visa status. This kind of golden opportunity looked great, and because I was from a Third World Nation, I thought I should grab the chance, no matter the reason.

But I sent on to decline this sudden, golden opportunity offered and with some sorrow, I kept focused on returning to Sri Lanka. The agent was very surprised, "What a foolish decision to make! I have never met someone who would decline such a golden offer."

I knew this was a suddenly from Satan who did not want me to pursue the Lord's leading in my life. If I had taken that offer, all that God has done in me and through me in Sri Lanka may have never happened. The girls' home, the national youth movement, so many lives saved, healed, delivered, and walking in God's purposes and destiny, the Bible school training and equipping for a new generation, missions, regional and national level victories, all would probably never have occurred to this extent!

As the Bible says, "God was looking for a man to go for Him." I chose to be that man, and today so many lives have been forever impacted because I obeyed.

In addition, to having the joy to see the Kingdom of God expanding, I also have shared the joy of knowing my success story has encouraged people around the world. I will receive my U.S. citizenship in a couple of years as part of God's plan for my life plan. He restored doublefold what I had given up.

I had zero in my hands, no church support and zero finances to my name. But I had something more valuable than material things and gold, I was full of fire, vision, faith, and joy. The only thing I had in my hands was a check for $500. Remember, I had just completed Bible school and like most students, we were facing the world with either none or very little resources. When I arrived in Sri Lanka, I tried to cash the $500 check but it bounced. This was a failure in the eyes of the people who do not understand but in the eyes of our Mighty God, I was facing a successful future.

Chapter 4

In Your Face Praying

The evil bow before the good and the wicked at the gates of the righteous.
Proverbs 14:19

Spiritual warfare

Two men came to the gate of 42/3 Galpotta Road in Rajagiriya, a large suburb of Colombo. The house we were renting was next to the church. They wanted me to pay them for informing me that the building we purchased for the church was up for sale. We knew about it because we lived next door to it. I refused to pay them as they had not done anything that warranted them being paid. They threatened me, "The Buddhists in the community have been talking about shooting you with a gun."

Instantly I became bold. I stretched my hands towards them, "The man of God does not leave this community but you will have to." I started to pray loudly and strong in unknown tongues given to me by Holy Spirit. Shocked, they both immediately had a look of fear. Horror showed on their faces. While I continued to blast them by praying loudly in tongues, they slowly walked to their tuk yuk (3-wheeler taxi) and drove away, never to return. It was like a slow-motion movie was playing right before me. Personally, I believe they may have seen angels as soon as I started praying in tongues. The look of profound horror and terror showed they were seeing somebody standing by me that was not visible to man's eye. Hearing me pray in a language they did not understand caused them to become extremely startled and fearful. When I saw them at a later time, they looked very sheepish and never confronted us, ever again.

About a year prior to the incident, I was led to make declarations at the gates of our church and our home which were standing side by side on the same lane. "The evil bow before the good, and the wicked at the gates of the righteous" (Proverbs 14:19). This was a rhema word from the Lord. A rhema word is a direct, living word. We kept declaring this daily, weekly, monthly, and from time to time when directed.

Changing the spiritual atmosphere
On another occasion near the entrance to the church about 30 young men forcibly dragged two of our young leaders to the road and were threatening to beat them. When I arrived, the young leaders were surrounded by this mob. My heart sank. Immediately Holy Spirit said, "Pray aloud in tongues." I obeyed and started praying

aloud in tongues. I walked toward the mob, instantaneously they became totally quiet. The crowd opened up and made room for me to walk into the middle, and then the crowd closed around us again. I continued to pray boldly in tongues.

Then I spoke to them in one sentence, and followed it with a sentence in tongues. I did this several times not showing any fear even though I was trembling on the inside. Then I instructed my two young men, "Now do what I'm doing, pray loudly in tongues, and follow me out." I shook the leader's hand while he was standing in front of the crowd. Praying, the two young men followed me away. When the boisterous crowd realized that we had walked out, they started to follow us. Immediately, without our knowledge the police were coming, they appeared, and the crowd disappeared into the night. It was a setup to cause trouble and the police were informed by the ring leader who wanted to intimidate us.

Angel armies
Our "in your face praying" "changed the spiritual atmosphere and released mighty angels to assist us. No one could lay a hand on us to hurt us. Praying in tongues is an incredibly powerful weapon that is available to use in battle, especially in areas where hostile and violent persecution is prevalent. Many times, believers are embarrassed and uncomfortable about engaging this weapon, and they are beaten or overwhelmed by hostile persecution. We should use it very powerfully, and it will help summon angel armies to come to assist us so we

can either make a strategic getaway or go on to fulfill our assignment courageously and victoriously.

We have implemented in your face praying countless numbers of times, and each time our attackers have retreated and even run away in great haste or even disappeared into hiding. We realized each time we came up against our enemies with in your face praying especially under great physical threat, the atmosphere around us was shifted and changed to make way for angel armies to invade our surroundings. As a result, the fear of God would fall upon our persecutors. Even though we were in a place of risking our lives, it was so awesome to watch and realize what the Lord was doing. The demonic forces using these demonized people were becoming weaker and worn down gradually until the people became timid and terrified themselves. Our aim was not to get into a clash, but a spiritual power encounter was playing outright before our eyes. It was absolutely wonderful to literally stumble into this revelation and use this secret spiritual weapon. God was starting to suddenly take charge of the atmosphere in a very genuine way and control all who were within that sphere. Praise the Lord! We do serve an Almighty God, and demons truly have to tremble and shudder.

This is what happened (Luke 4:28-30) when Jesus was furiously driven out of town to be thrown down from the cliff. The Scripture says "But He walked right through the crowd and went on His way." The overwhelming shift in the atmosphere happened, and the people were overpowered by the presence of angel armies. They became meek as lambs and could do nothing to carry on with their sudden violent intentions. Wow!!! We have experienced this type of scenarios many, many times in our journey.

Some people don't believe these testimonies are true or don't know what to do with this explanation. But those who have believed and acted on these hidden strategies have also discovered similar types of miraculous deliverances and protection. Our experience is that in your face praying is a way for Holy Spirit to push our prayers up against the enemy's face when he tries to come up against us.

Chapter 5

Regional Corporate Prayer Journey

> I have posted watchmen on your walls,
> Jerusalem. They will never be silent day or
> night. You who call on the Lord give
> yourselves no rest, and give him no rest til
> he establishes Jerusalem and makes her
> the praise of the earth.
>
> Isaiah 62:6-7

As I served as a pastor who founded and pioneered a church in July 1991, after few years I had a strong desire to invite Christian ministers to join together to pray. I felt like the gathering would include pastors and leaders of ministries in Sri Jayawardenepura Kotte, the official capital of Sri Lanka. I sensed that if we would pray together something greater could happen in the region. There was a sensing that we could do more together than each one could do separately.

Starting in 1995, from time to time I began to gather the pastors and leaders to a prayer breakfast at our church and at other churches as well. This gathering took place at least about three to four times a year.

By the year 2000, a group of pastors in our region had watched the Transformation 1 video produced by The Sentinel Group. A series of documentaries were compiled by a noted missions and revival sign post reader. The award-winning documentaries have been viewed by 250+ million. About six pastors along with me had been greatly challenged by the message of these videotaped testimonies showing the importance of persevering prayer showing how transformation was taking place. The obedient action led to four cities experiencing a degree of spiritual and societal transformation. The seven of us made a dedication and commitment to gather together monthly to pray, eat and fellowship. In June 2000 we held our first interchurch prayer rally in a historical mainline church building very close to the Parliament of the Democratic Socialist Republic of Sri Lanka, the supreme legislative body. Approximately 80 people from ten churches attended to worship and pray together. It was a very exciting beginning.

The pastors continued to meet monthly at our church along with several other churches in the region. To maintain consistency, however, it was necessary for me and a couple of other pastors to coordinate these monthly gatherings. There was no official leader, but it was a collaborative ministry of volunteers with an initiative to build the prayer effort. We were becoming

Kingdom minded not empire minded, so we decided not to seek titles or positions. We were convinced that the more and more we gathered to pray, we would see awakening, revival and transformation in our society. Pastors and leaders continue to meet monthly and gather together for a corporate prayer rally once a year. At times we even do all night worship and intercession rallies. Gathering together from May 2000 for 18 years, we are going strong. In addition to praying for the church and kingdom of God to advance in our region and nation, we also prayed for aspiring political and business leaders and encourage them to get involved in the process of transformation in their spheres of influence. Our position is that we need the spiritual leadership converging with the leadership of the government and economic spheres in particular in order for the region to see an awakening taking place.

Some of the notable results from the regional 18-year, prayer initiative

1. A greater sense of unity among pastors and churches of our region; Kotte, Maharagama, Kaduwela, and Colombo. This is the region where the administrative capital of Sri Lanka is situated.
2. The monthly prayer gathering bonded the pastors and leaders together as they prayed and ministered to each other.
3. The 27-year long ethnic, civil war ended in 2009. Over 100,000 died. We did our part together for many years with prayers and making declaration that God would bring the civil strife to an end.

And He did! Other networks were also interceding. The Body of Christ prayed and saw good results!

4. From 2000 to 2009, all terrorist activities ceased in the KMK (our) region after we started gathering together for united,intentional corporate prayer from year 2000. Meanwhile, explosive terrorism continued to rage in other parts of the nation until 2009.

5. The anti-conversion legislation, especially targeting Christians, was defeated three times during the period of 2000 to 2017. It was brought up but did not succeed in passing.

6. Kotte and the surrounding region has rapidly developed. Tall buildings, housing, government institutions and offices, highway overpass bridges, walking strips, and recreational sites are in noticeable view.

7. Corruption, fraud and injustice is beginning to be addressed more intentionally.

8. Very, very hostile anti-Christian forces are starting to wear down and is weakening, little by little.

9. The monthly prayer initiatives along with some other prayer efforts have shifted the nation's political climate and brought in a new president, prime minister and government in 2015. Against all impossibilities, a new era has dawned.

10. Some conservative believers were voted into parliament or appointed to influential positions.

When the battle was raging, we increased our prayer efforts to include doing warfare prayer in the Sri Lanka Parliament, the Supreme Court, the city and municipal councils, and other strategic places. We did many prayer walks, prayer drives and prayer journeys. This resulted in an overturning or stalling of unjust laws or bills.

A stronger prayer authority is released when spiritual leaders unite and pray over their cities, regions and nations. When they make prophetic decrees and declarations, strongholds come down and demonic structures are dismantled. Scripture records, "One shall chase 1,000 and two a 10,000" (Deuteronomy 32:30). When they do it over and over again, it is not a one-time event but an ongoing journey toward pulling down, uprooting, planting, and building, they begin to see the fruit of the city and regional transformation taking place. This is how kingdom-minded leaders are to function. Satan tries to keep spiritual leaders divided and from embarking on a journey together for awakening, revival and transformation.

I encourage every leader and believer to take this secret to heart and begin your own journey toward community, city and nation transformation.

As a regional prayer network, we did our part. God heard and did the rest!!

Chapter 6

A Voice for the Voiceless

Speak up for those who cannot speak for themselves, for the rights of all who are destitute.

Proverbs 31:8

February 28, 2000, we officially opened Shepherds Heart Childrens Home on Galpotta Road, Nawala, Sri Lanka. A visiting Christian musician and minister who is known as a gospel music pioneer did the ribbon cutting to open the home. The facility comprised of three rooms, a small living room, and a little kitchen. It was on the floor above the large house where Overcomers Church would be located.

In November 2001 three little girls who were siblings came to live at Shepherds Heart. My wife Melanie and I agreed Shepherds Heart would be a haven and refuge for abandoned or at risk young girls. We decided that a safe place should be available for these precious, innocent young lives. We had a caring, loving woman who is affectionately called, "Mama A."

The small girls lived in the home for only three months, but their mother who was living a very rough life wanted them back unexpectedly. While living with her mother, the youngest who was about four years old fell into an unguarded water well and died. This tragic incident provoked us all the more to carry out the vision for rescuing at-risk children from impending disaster.

In late 2002, two girls, came to live at Shepherds Heart. One was 12 1/2 and the other was 2. They have lived in the home their entire lives. During the past 15 years, others have joined us, from time to time. It was extremely difficult for the girls when any of the girls left the home for whatever reason. It was heart breaking and lots of tears have been shed. Our home has been established as family-style so everyone bonds together like a family. When a child leaves, it was like a tearing off of the emotional fabric. When visitors come, the children always ask, "When are you coming back to see us?" They love visitors, and it brings them great joy.

In 2003, Shepherds Heart was renting a house next door to Overcomers Church. Suddenly, it was put up for sale in the newspapers without any prior notice from the owner. Soon people were stopping by to see the house. The owner sheepishly admitted that he had decided to sell. We immediately decided to purchase the house and property, though we had no money, and banks and other organizations would not lend to our small nonprofit.

We arrived in the U.S to hopefully raise a sizable amount for a down payment and pay the balance over a period of time. It was a David and Goliath moment. I decided I wasn't leaving the U.S until we saw a breakthrough or received a clear word that the large amount would be met. This was a big challenge, and then to top it all, I had a visit from a demon one morning. I woke up around 6 am to a very disturbing experience. The room became dark, and I felt immobilized and weak. I was in a daze! I sensed a voice telling me, "I am going to kill you!" Somehow, I dragged myself out to the living room and was still in a daze. I began praying to dislodge the spirit. After about an hour, Melanie came in to the living room. She woke up, "Honey, I had an awful dream." I replied, "I know that's why I'm out here praying." Together we prayed and prayed, and gradually the demonic presence was driven away from us. It was an unforgettable experience! We were on a journey and learning to exercise our faith and authority in overcoming the giants we were facing.

After we returned, no matter how hard we tried, we were falling back on our payments, which was to be completed in one year. The house owner decided to seek another party. But finally, he sold to us at a slightly lower price saying "Your God gave me a severe, unbearable back pain. I decided to complete the sale." The fear of God was all over him, and he wanted to be completely free. In 2004, we came into ownership. "If God is for us, who can be against us?" (Romans 8:31).

The house was a three-room, one-story facility. About seven years later, the decision was made to demolish the house and build a three-story building for Shepherds Heart Childrens Home. Again, this was a bigger project than earlier. A huge amount was needed, over $250,000. In our world where we continually struggle to make monthly budget, this was a big mountain to climb. We had less than 10% in hand. But somehow, we had an unexplainable faith and confidence that God would supply.

However, two days after we laid the foundation stones, Woody had a heart attack and was in the Intensive Care Unit for eight days. Overcomers Church and many, many other dear people close by and across the globe prayed him through. Even the atheist, Buddhist surgeon was very, very surprised and amazed at the response. As Woody lay waiting, the angiogram was performed, and results showed that his arteries were blocked 100%. One week later, the arteries suddenly relaxed and opened up remarkably. The surgeon expressed her surprise, "Your arteries are much better. We could do stents instead of going for a bypass surgery." Woody exclaimed, "Thank you, Jesus!" She retorted, "What about us?" I quickly replied, "I was thanking God for gifted people like you." I was on the operating table with all the hookups in place as she questioned me. She seemed calmer after that statement. Later she said "Nobody has made me change my decision in how I dealt with my patients. You are the only person who has done it, and it worked out better." This particular incident opened the door for us to have an ongoing conversation on the topic of the existence of a living, loving God.

The three-story building for the girls was completed 18 months later. The city council gave the building permit approval, but five months later withdrew the approval. The reason was that the Buddhist monks are against the city council granting the approval. Buddhism is the national religion, and they believed conversions may take place; therefore, they opposed it. In nations like Sri Lanka, this is how human rights are grossly violated. Even though Sri Lanka is a signatory to the United Nations Declaration of Human Rights and citizens in Sri Lanka are entitled to freedom of religion, this injustice is widely practiced. This is especially true toward Christians who are working to rebuild broken, destitute lives. We finally received our building permit approval 5 1/2 years later, and that was with paying a fine because we would not resort to bribing the mayor, the councilors or officials.

The good news was that even with only partial approval of the building permit, the council did not interfere with the construction of the three-story building. The council not interfering with the ongoing construction was unusual! The ministry implemented ongoing intercession two to three times every day. While the construction continued for 18 months, Nehemiah's strategy with building the walls of Jerusalem was our goal. Throughout the day, the Israelite workers had construction tools in one hand, and a sword in the other. They worked and prayed. We followed the same strategy, and the enemy's plans were utterly defeated. Many wonderful, faithful people supported us during this very challenging time of opposition and resistance.

We received the all-important official children's home, known as a child development center, government registration after 14 long years duration. I know this sounds unbelievable, but this is how things go in many nations that practice religious persecution against Christians.

Enormous challenges exist in our predominantly Buddhist nation with less than 2% evangelical Christians. The Department of Probation and Childcare is controlled by the Buddhist government system. Shepherds Heart Childrens Home must abide by all government regulations which includes logging all daily activities, and incidents with each girl. Documents must be recorded about food and illness. Any travel out and in including delays and reasons for such delays, personal injury, etc., are also documented. The government provides no financial support, medical support or other social services. The total burden is on the home's management.

When each girl reaches age 19, legally they are required to be released from Shepherds Heart and from the government department's system. Ready or not, the girls are required to leave! However, after going through the trauma and brokenness in their lives, they are not prepared to face challenges and decisions that society places on them and what is required to live normal lives. Proper preparation and equipping for transition must take place intentionally so all the sacrificial loving care and efforts provided for the girls are not lost. Statistics globally have proven that when a child has "aged out" of the safe environment, they often become victims of unfortunate circumstances.

After much concern and discussions, a separate, external stairway was built for girls who reach 19 years. The stairway provides access to the third floor where they are living. The two entities are completely separate. The third floor has been named Deborah Court. The plan worked! The department was pleased with the new arrangement and granted the approval to continue. Several Christian homes have been closed down or compelled to close due to the unjust, draconian-type system and challenges faced. We understand the necessity of government requirements, but sometimes they "go overboard," and people with good intentions cannot navigate the system. However, when the Lord gives vision, He also provides a way to navigate the path to success. He is our awesome God!

Daily devotions and prayer
Daily at 5:15 am and 6:30 pm, our girls who live at Shepherds Heart meet in their prayer room for worship, prayer and devotions. They love singing together and prayer. They played musical instruments and the older girls take turns leading devotions and prayer.

It is normal when people arrive at Shepherd's Heart to hear the joyful, passionate singing and sounds coming from young voices. They were learning to overcome the grief and sorrow and enjoy the Lord's presence and each other.

Testimonies from the Shepherd's Heart family.

- Two of our girls have performed excellently at the General Certificate of Education ordinary level examinations. One had eight A's, and the other had seven A's and one B. This level is the equivalent of the 11th grade.
- Several won certificates and trophies for excellence in academics and performance.
- Even though a few have had difficulties and could not pass at high school level, they have gone onto earning Harvest Leadership Institute Bible school diplomas and a Certificate in Advance Graphic Designing. Our objective is to prepare each girl to live a successful adult life.
- The girls have learned to play the guitar, keyboards, singing and leading worship, served in Overcomers Church children's ministry and SuperHeroes Pre-school, greeting and ushering, and serving where ever there has been a need.
- Our oldest girl, Rasangi, serves as Melanie's assistant and does most of the graphic design for ministry brochures, advertisements and invitations, and she is a leader for her youth group. She also serves in Overcomers Church Media Department.
- The second oldest, Nalani, worked at the local YWCA. She received a scholarship to attend Texas Bible Institute in Columbus, Texas. After she graduates the one-year program, she will attend Christ For The Nations Institute, Dallas, Texas, on a work-study scholarship.
- Chandima is working as an administrative assistant at Woody's office. She leads the Sinhala

Congregation children's ministry that has over 30 children.

- Champa was selected to give a speech before 3,000 people on International Children's Day on October 1, 2014. She was selected from some of the top students in the area. The nation's leader, President Rajapakse, and other dignitaries were present.
- Harshani was selected to be the head prefect which is the student head leader of her school.
- Shepherds Heart Childrens Home has received compliments and is said to be one of the most excellently managed children's homes by the Department of Probation and Childcare in Sri Lanka.
- Regularly Shepherds Heart Childrens Home receives visits from every day people as well as high-level dignitaries and Sri Lankan cabinet ministers. They hear the singing about the love of Christ and prayers. All of them have been refreshed with the beautiful, loving atmosphere.

We are proud of our young ladies! Two students, Marion and Lindianne, who placed in the top 5%. 275,000+ in Senior Secondary Schools nationally took the exam. Marion placed No. 407 in her district and 1,459 in the island, out of 275,000+. We are thankful to the Lord for their achievements. They are also very involved in Overcomers Church activities.

All of us who have poured our lives into Shepherds Heart Childrens Home are very proud of our girls, the management and house parents. We are amazed to see them growing up to become risk takers and confident young ladies. They have been trained in biblical values and are not intimidated by others. They know what they believe and Who they believe in. "Train up a child in the way he should go" (Proverbs 22:6).

Many have contributed and supported in the success of Shepherds Heart and the girls. Our administrative staff and caregivers, the board of directors, local and overseas volunteers, and precious donors have blessed the ministry in so many amazing ways.

This vision to provide a safe haven for the girls began with very little, but God has made us faithful stewards of the increase He has brought our way. When we are faithful in the little things, He will give us the opportunity to be faithful stewards in the greater.

Chapter 7

Police Traffic Gloves

I went to the city gates and took my place
in the public square.

Job 29:7

The story of Overcomers Church connecting with the police department of our city, Rajagiriya, is an incredible, unimaginable one. We believe if we are to be an influence for positive change, it is necessary to find ways to connect with our city and region in a tangible, practical way. From the time I started to pioneer and pastor Overcomers Church, I reached out to build relations with the police and other important agencies who were Buddhist in nature because all systems were operated by Buddhists. I would introduce myself to the police chief and give a gift of a John Maxwell leadership book or a plaque with leadership guidelines and converse with them. As the police chiefs kept changing frequently every two to three years, I would repeat the same process when the change would take place.

Usually the police departments operated by Buddhists are known to be extremely unfriendly and hostile towards churches and believers. Therefore, they support the monks and mobs that persecute the church. When the churches were facing the mobs that had arrived to beat the pastors and believers, destroy instruments and equipment, and setting the church buildings on fire, they would not respond to cries for help by the pastors. If they did, they arrived at the church only when persecutors had dispersed, and the injured had been hospitalized. Or if they arrived when the mob was inciting violence, typically they would become onlookers and refrained from intervening like they would normally do. We, at Overcomers Church, faced much harassment and persecution for many, many past years before the 2008 December police initiative. The police would even walk in with guns loaded in our prayer gathering to intimidate, supposedly doing building checks with false claims that we were hiding or training terrorists. This enabled them to tear up our sacred prayer times. However, we ended up laying hands on them and praying for them. They would leave shamefacedly, shrug their shoulders and feel hot beneath the collar from embarrassment. I would call the police chief the following day and thank him for sending his men to visit our services.

Cookies at Christmas

In 2008 December Melanie's Grandma, Alice Gorter, came down for a visit with her mother Norma and relatives. We had already made plans with the police for the church to do a 10-minute, mini-carol service and to give Christmas goodies to the force. Grandma at 85 years led a team and baked 850 delicious cookies for the police. After we sang and handed out the cookies and cakes, the police served us tea and biscuits. They were absolutely amazed, "Nobody, comes to do anything good for us. They only come to complain, grumble and accuse. We have never had anyone do what your church has done. And with no hidden agenda as well. There was a shift in the attitudes and hearts of the police as well as the atmosphere.

A great door has been opened. The following year in November 2009, I (Woody) and Melanie were driving through the city. I noticed that the policemen giving directions for traffic were not visible, especially at nighttime as they had no bright reflector gloves to use. Their dark hands were not visible, and the traffic was in utter confusion and chaos. Holy Spirit whispered in my ear, "You notice the confusion and the chaos. How about donating traffic reflector gloves this Christmas to the police?" I replied, "What would that do? Could we do something like that." Holy Spirit replied, "Just donate, and watch what I will do."

We discussed this subject with the police and got 30 pairs made by the official manufacturer of gloves. We donated them that December 2009 and saw a major shift take place. The police chief was overwhelmed and dragged me into his office, "How did you know that we needed them badly? Our budgets were so depleted, we couldn't even afford to buy gloves." Who are you? We never met a church like this before? Could we work together?" I explained, "We noticed your policemen were having trouble directing traffic without the proper gear. We decided to donate them." We were invited to sit on an advisory committee for the police to represent the Christian community of our city.

> When a man's ways please the Lord, He makes even his enemies be at peace with him.
>
> Proverbs 16:7

This police advisory committee meets monthly for an hour to discuss crime, violence, drugs, racial, religious issues, and other relevant items. The committee includes the police chief, other religious leaders, dignitaries, etc.

Giving keeps the door open
Overcomers Church continues to care for the police by giving and blessing them regularly at our annual December police carols. We gave to meet critical needs. Traffic reflector gloves, vests, mattresses, cubical blinds, computers and printers, large fans, cookies, cakes, mugs, and umbrellas. Regular giving also helped keep the doors opened. This financial contribution is minimal but valuable for building the relationship. A retired police officer from Dallas heard our story and supported the

police initiative in Sri Lanka financially and with prayer. She would contribute annually for several years because she knew the importance of reaching and influencing. This is a challenging arena! After retirement, she even visited Sri Lanka and met with our police department.

Intentionally, we prepare a financial budget for the police initiative so we were ready. We treat this initiative as a very important annual event, and make plans to be ready. Regional transformational work cannot be a one-time event. It may begin with a one-time, major breakthrough, but it must be stewarded carefully to see tangible, growing, lasting change.

Major shift produced ongoing results

1. We were invited to represent the Christian community on the police advisory committee.
2. We are invited to pray at important public interpolice gatherings where 10 to 12 stations come together in assembly numbering hundreds. The hundreds were primarily Buddhists.
3. When the Muslims, approximately 9%, of our city were agitating and restless, we were invited as pastors and representatives of the police advisory committee to accompany the police to be mediators and peace makers. No other religious leader was invited.
4. When national level fraud and corruption was investigated, we were invited officially to be observers of the proceedings.

5. Police sought our help to find an elders' home when elderly destitute persons were directed to them by the courts.
6. When Buddhist monks openly criticized our church before the advisory committee, the police officers defended the church and helped silence the critics publicly. Very unusual!
7. Every Christmas we have the honor of praying and making prophetic declarations in the police station over the microphone before a Buddhist police force of about 250.
8. The police requested Overcomers Church on December 2, 2017 to help decorate the police station for Christmas. This was a first time! The station is usually especially dull around Christmas.
9. In 2014 when one of the police chiefs was scheming and backstabbing Overcomers Church people, He was arrested and thrown in prison. The Buddhist policemen said to us, "It was because he was opposing the church that he was imprisoned." Our public prophetic declarations were making a powerful impact. He was imprisoned for being supportive of the drug trade, but some of the policemen knew that the spirit of God was working.
10. A group of policemen came to us to hear the Gospel and to receive prayer.
11. The Buddhist police provides help annually to direct traffic at our Christmas eve and December 31, watch-night services. Because the people are

joyful and the church is full along with visitors, in the past those have been potential times for persecution from Buddhists.

12. Currently, the persecutors are reluctant to persecute or bring opposition against Overcomers Church, because of the tight relationship that exists between the police and our people. We follow protocol with dress, behavior, language, etc., to help maintain dignity and respect so our dealings with the police are esteemed.

In a nation where Christianity is less than 2% of a 22 million, we must develop divine strategies to penetrate and work among the lost and opposed. God gives wisdom and strategy and gives open doors for the Kingdom gospel to advance.

Love your neighbor as yourself.
Matthew 22:39

Chapter 8

Facing and Overcoming Persecution

Put on the whole armor of God, that you
may be able to stand against the wiles of
the devil.

Ephesians 6:11

Sri Lanka is a nation where Christianity is less than 2% of
the population, a total of 22 million people. As a small
minority group, persecutions toward the Gospel and the
Church is to be more than to be expected.

I know the information about Buddhist
nationalism may surprise some of the readers, but it is
important for Christians to have a better understanding
of the radicalism of Buddhism in Sri Lanka. As a man who
grew up in this atmosphere, it is a culture that is very
much involved in our everyday lives even in our
educational systems. Christians, like us, have had to walk
through extremely tough, dangerous experiences to

increase church planting and establishing evangelism. Believers in our nation cannot be weak or "sitting on the fence." I praise God that I have learned many lessons from the generation that pioneered before me.

Stoning the Church

The Sunday service had been closed for the day, and many had been touched by Holy Spirit. One believer informed me that a neighbor wished to speak to me. "The whole community wants to stone this church, if you don't cease your activities," he spoke with anger. A stocky middle-aged, English-speaking Muslim man stood at the church's entrance with eyes blazing. I responded with an unusual calmness, "If that is what y'all are intending to do, then you need to go ahead and do what you have planned to do! I cannot do anything without speaking to my higher ups." He walked away angrily threatening to do what he said the community would do.

Starting with that moment, he started to harass our church. He would hang his underwear in a prominent place for the public to notice, look with a lustful, lewd manner at the women attending church as they had to pass his house, make loud distracting sounds to disturb the services, make constant threatening phone calls, and many other things to annoy those who were coming and going. He had mentioned to a mutual friend of ours, "When the church prays in tongues that really makes me angry." About a year later without any warning, his father died with a heart attack. Six months later, his mother died in the same way. He became very worried and fearful. Again, he wanted to know if the church would put a curse on any family that they did not like? The mutual friends he talked to replied the church does not curse people but only does blessings. About a year later this man while spending one evening on a sea beach south of Colombo with his girlfriend was confronted by robbers who wanted his gold chain and valuables. He tried fighting back but was stabbed in the back with a knife and died.

The whole community around the church was struck with fear and terror with the man's sudden death. A report was going around that the man who went up against the church is dead. Several people apologized, "Father, please don't be upset with us. We will meet you as we need your help" A Muslim cousin came to reside in the deceased neighbor's house but quickly came to make peace with us before moving in. The community stopped persecuting the church and allowed us to proceed with our work.

Just to give further clarification, the term *father* is used often as a way to respect church pastors and leaders. Used in the Roman Catholic tradition and non-Christians were familiar with this type of terminology. In a nation without a strong godly culture, superstition and curses are common in the daily lives of people.

Declaring Joshua 1:3

When Melanie and I moved to the rented house, next to the current location of the church, and learned the house and property were for sale. We decided to purchase it for the church. Because of the persecution, it is normal for churches to buy property with a building on it. This allows the church to function temporarily until they have "gained the ground." Building permits from the local councils are almost impossible to obtain for church buildings. When the land owner received a phone call from me about the purchase of the property, he refused to sell to us. He informed me, "The community does not want the church to have it."

We regrouped with our leaders and received direction from Holy Spirit that the seven of our key leaders were to walk around the property seven times declaring Joshua 1:3, "Every place that the sole of your foot will tread upon I have given you." We declared this Scripture over and over again, anointed the property with oil and changed the spiritual atmosphere that night. Repeating the promise and giving it a prophetic expression built our faith to keep going forward. When I called the owner the following day, he was very willing to sell the property to us with no objections whatsoever. Overnight a night-and-day change had taken place in his heart. "The king's heart is in the hand of the Lord. He turns it whichever way He pleases (Proverbs 21:1).

The prophetic *now* dream

In November 2003, Melanie and I were in Jackson, Mississippi, staying at a pastor's home ready to speak on Sunday. The threat of persecution was particularly high in Sri Lanka. Buddhist monks were militantly leading mobs to vandalize and burn down church buildings. The monks along with the mobs were beating pastors and believers to force them to close down churches and completely leave the areas.

The dream that Friday night was one like no other! A Buddhist monk with a hand raised, surrounded by a mob was threatening to attack me. It appeared to be like nighttime. I woke up trembling and sweating profusely. I could not go back to sleep again. Early the following morning, I shared with my pastor friend that I needed to stay and pray, as I was very disturbed. From 7 am to 10 am, I interceded and warred in the spirit. I really did not know what was happening but was sensing great danger for Overcomers Church. There was no way to communicate instantly with the leaders so I was praying based upon the prompting of Holy Spirit.

That very hour a notorious militant monk together with several other monks and a gang of men had arrived at the church and demanded the security guard to open up the door. Pastor Kumar who leads the Sinhala congregation and Pastor Sumithra who had been in the vicinity joined to stop them. When they received the news, they persuaded the monks and the gang to refrain from damaging and torching down the building. It appeared as though the fear of God was invading the place. Even though the monk gang was on the property for an entire hour, and usually would have done much damage, they could not succeed in their evilness. Finally, they departed taking from the office a few worship CDs and a file with the believers contact information. We were happy about the possibility of monks listening to worship music in their Buddhist temples.

Later when I checked the time that it happened, I was interceding for three hours in Mississippi at the very same time the gang of monks had been at church. I was 10,000 miles away from the very grave danger, but it was defeated with God's early warning systems. God can reveal to you by His spirit, even though it is 10,000 miles away, and have you pray victory over the dangerous situation your church is experiencing. The spiritual atmosphere was changed and angel armies intervened to strike terror and confusion so the attackers were weakened and confused causing them to depart without any success. Just like when the Amalekites suddenly attacked Israel in the desert without any warning. As Moses stood with arms raised on a hill, Aaron and Hur supported him with tireless intercession. Joshua overpowered and defeated the nation of Amalek completely (Exodus 17:8-13). This was also like Elisha knowing what the Syrian army was planning to do to Israel many hundreds of miles away. (2 Kings 6:8-10.)

For about 15 years, that particular monk, Venerable Gnanasara, has led many violent attacks against many churches and believers. This firebrand monk is just like a continuation of Saul's persecution of the Church in the New Testament. Our prayer is that this enemy will have a similar conversion where Saul had an encounter with the Lord on his Damascus road journey. His name was changed to Paul, and he taught the Gospel to the world during the first century.

A few years later we were able to have an opportunity to share the gospel with this particular monk and plant seeds for the Kingdom of God. Prayer pierces through spiritual darkness and brings light. He appeared to be somewhat ashamed and sheepish which was very unusual, because he had been unsuccessful at fulfilling his very destructive mission.

Poster Persecution Campaign
In earlier years, 2001 through 2003, at 5 am corporate prayer was held at the church daily, and several would attend. On one of the days, I was the only one in attendance. As I waited in prayer, I sensed a leading by Holy Spirit to walk down the Galpotta Road, where the church is located. Actually, I felt an invisible hand on my back give me a push forward. No sooner did I take a few steps when I noticed a poster on our boundary wall. The words were full of hatred toward Overcomers Church. It proclaimed, "Let's all unite to drive out this dancing, troublesome church from our community." I ripped down the poster and proceeded further to tear down a number of posters displayed all the way down the road. Before daylight, all the posters were removed! I read one poster that was fueled with the wrath to attack.

We later learned that the instigators were astonished to learn that I had the leading to remove posters from the entire neighborhood before daylight set in. God showed us if we would simply obey, He would enable us to be always one step ahead on the enemy.

God's secret agents on a secret mission
Another occasion the City Municipal Council sent a threatening letter that they planned to demolish a part

of the church building because they wanted to persecute the church. The city councils were well known for doing such unjust and evil deeds. I sensed a leading from the Holy Spirit to take about five of our pastors and prayer walk the city council grounds. While we were there, Holy Spirit urged me, "Now, go into the chief engineer's office when he is out doing lunch and make prophetic declarations." Feeling very nervous and fearful, I chose to obey. I posted two of the pastors at the entrance with cell phones with instructions, "Call me as soon as he is driving in." Pastor Kumar and I armed ourselves with dark sunglasses, anointed the soles of our shoes with oil and walked into the office talking loudly. When the secretaries looked up inquiringly, we spoke to each other loudly in English. For non-English speakers, they became visibly uncomfortable. I spoke out, "We were told to wait till the chief engineer arrives." On hearing us, the secretaries went back to their work, and we charged in to his office. Two men were repairing a copier, and when they looked up, we repeated the same line for them to hear. They continued on with the repair. We looked around and started praying using our cell phones. It actually looked like we were phoning someone. We made declarations and broke the power of the spirit of the antichrist that was holding the chief engineer, and turning him against us. We had some anointing oil and anointed the office and furniture discreetly and released the presence and authority of the Lord in that office. We departed within five to ten minutes.

The entire scenario was like a secret agent on a secret mission. But what we did changed the spiritual atmosphere over the council. Seven days later, the threat against the Overcomers Church was completely nullified. God gave us the victory once again. We give God the glory for great things that he has done!

Furthermore, we were able to build a relationship with this official who was a one-time avowed fighter not only against Overcomers Church but the entire Church in the city. I had previously seen him authorize and carry out the demolition of another church building in the city, population 200,000. Now, we have the opportunity to visit him every Christmas to share Christmas goodies and discuss spiritual matters.

Chapter 9

Supernatural Wonders of God

These signs will accompany those who
believe…. They will place their hands on
the sick people, and they will get well.

                                   Mark 16:17-19

Two miracles within one week

On January 24, 1994, a woman had arrived to speak with
me. Her life was in absolute shambles. Little did I realize
the important role she would play in years to come.
Sumithra had spent time in prison and tried to commit
suicide several times. Even with this morning visit she
had been directed by a 10-year-old girl to meet me. She
had seen this young girl at a bus stop and had shared
part of her painful story. The girl and the mother had

visited the church a few times. In fact, Sumithra never saw the girl again. At Overcomers Church we also did not see the girl. It is one of those unexplainable mysteries but out of it came a Divine appointment.

After listening to Sumithra talk about her life for a while, I shared the Gospel with her, and she received Christ and was born again into the Kingdom of God. The Bible in John 3 discusses Nicodemus and his born-again experience. This is the type of experience that Sumitra had. The first miracle was when Sumithra became born again. As a normal practice, I handed her a Bible in the Sinhala language and invited her to read it from that day forward. With tears in her eyes she replied, "I cannot see to read any longer." This was a real problem, but I coerced her to go home and try reading by faith daily until her eye sight was restored. Shaking her head in disbelief, she said she would try. The next morning after a short prayer, she opened her newly acquired Bible and tried reading. However, she could read nothing at all. She tried the second day, the third and the fourth to no avail. But by the fifth day when she opened the Bible, her heart began to beat with excitement. She could hardly make out letters. It was as though looking through holes that looked like pin pricks. By the sixth day, the cloud over her eyes cleared, and she was reading really well. This was the second miracle. It has been 24 years since and not only has she defied medical science but also studied and preached from the Word of God for many, many years to various congregations. Her testimony of healing and restoration of her life was even shared on several national TV channels, and many have been touched by her story. Today she pastors her own congregation and is used greatly in evangelism. She is also involved in planting new house churches.

Symptoms do not determine our condition

Another young lady, Candi, had committed to serving full-time in ministry at Overcomers Church. From the very onset, she would experience severe back issues that caused her to be laid up in bed for two to three days a week. When we would pray the prayer of faith and healing over her, she would fully recover. But when she returned home, she would relapse once again. This happened several times, over and over again for months. Her conditions were very serious, and doctors said it was a prolapse of the discs in her spinal area. The only solution was a surgery that could be performed in the USA for a colossal amount.

I realized that every time the symptoms were experienced, she surrendered and allow herself to be overcome by the condition. I encouraged her to learn to resist and go into spiritual war against the condition to maintain her healing. Soon she was able to recover fully and now remains totally healed. Sixteen years later, God has used her mightily with children and in several other areas of ministry. "Submit to God, resist the devil and he will flee from you" (James 4:7).

In many Third World nations people from the other faiths that do not believe in God need to see supernatural healing, deliverances, signs and wonders to turn to God. It is common in ungodly culture to see the supernatural of dark forces and manifestations of the demonic through the occult, witchcraft and false worship. I have seen people within temples literally getting possessed by demons and manifestations going on for hours. Seeing God's supernatural power accompanying with preaching of His word with miracles, and signs and wonders is convincing to those who do not believe in our God. To see something greater that is powerful and lasting open doors for them to turn to God and become followers of Christ.

24/7 prayer watch

Chandi turned to Christ from a mix of two non-Christian faiths. Particularly, because she saw her severely oppressed mother turn to Christ and receive deliverance but also seeing Jesus appear to her in a dream. In the dream she heard Jesus say, "Be converted and be baptized." And that is what she did! She repented and believed in the Lord. She even went on to Bible school in the UK and at Harvest Leadership Institute. She is ministering alongside her husband Herron pastoring a new church plant and other ministry to advance the Kingdom of God.

After several years, she had married one of our pastors, Herron. After the marriage, she gave birth to their daughter Ahnya. The delivery took place by C-section. However, because of an allergic reaction from the anesthesia, she went in to a coma and remained unconscious and on a ventilator for seven whole days. However, the baby was healthy and doing quite well. We consulted together and decided to mobilize the entire congregation to pray on-site at the hospital and in the

Intensive Care Unit, when permitted, until she regained consciousness. It was a grueling battle! Night and day prayer was prayed over Chandi. The surgeons were almost paralyzed not knowing what to do. They were without answers! Just like in the book of Acts where the church prayed continuously for Peter to be released from prison, we prayed for Chandi to be delivered from a spirit of death.

Finally, on the seventh day she opened her eyes, regained consciousness and started on the long road to recovery. The Buddhist surgeons admitted, "If you did not do what you did the last seven days, we believe the outcome would have been very different." The surgeons also inquired about Overcomers Church and were open to discuss spiritual matters.

Dreams still lead people to Christ
Just like God used a dream to help Chandi make a firm decision to serve God, a Muslim man also received a dream where he saw Jesus appear to Him and calling him to come to Him. His wife who had been a Buddhist was a believer for some years. I asked her if she was praying for her husband's salvation. She replied, "He's a Muslim. This could never ever happen." I encouraged her, "If you as a Buddhist could turn to Christ, why not your husband also?" Reluctantly she decided to give it a try. About a year later, her husband in his mid 60's had a dream about Jesus appearing to him dressed like a shepherd, like in the Bible, "Don't be afraid to come to me as I have a plan for your life and I want to bless you." With abundant tears and much sobbing, he gave his life

to Christ at an evangelistic service, was baptized and served the Lord until he went home to Jesus 15 years later in December of 2016. From time to time, he would often receive dreams of Jesus appearing to him, and with tears and great emotion he would share them with us. I believe he was also impacted indirectly by the prayers that were made for Muslims by the millions of intercessors worldwide.

As Overcomers Church and the ministry continued to see the Kingdom of God advance, some in the immediate community became fearful and insecure. To give themselves a false security, they started to set up statues of their gods close to the church to intimidate us. It went from wooden altars to concrete altars, and they offered daily sacrifices. We continued to make room for God's presence to saturate the area through several 72-hour and 48-hour, ongoing, uninterrupted worship and intercession gatherings. The statues and concrete altars were totally ripped out of the ground and removed from the area by the people themselves, never more to return. This is highly unusual as the altars are a symbol of possessing the land for their gods. It was very similar to Dagon's statues that were unable to sit enthroned by the Ark of the Covenant, no matter how many times they tried to set them up (1 Samuel 5:1-4).

Witch doctor leaves town for good
The witch doctor had been mesmerizing the community for many years. When Overcomers Church moved into the area in April 2001, the witch doctor used his god house as the center from which to mobilize the radical,

hostile Buddhist community to oppose the Christians and the church in various ways. They would blast the church with hate speech over loud speakers throughout the community. Hundreds gathered to make plans to literally drive out the church out of the area.

A number of years later the wife of the witch doctor was very upset with him and beat him on the head severely, tore down the display signs of the shrine, took the two sons and departed. She never returned. A year later, he sold the place to a buyer and secretly departed at night time when he would not be seen. The new owner has built a house on that location and plans to live there.

Our ministry has seen how changing the spiritual atmosphere through worship, intercession, prayer walking, faith, and patience has worn down the demonic powers and thus compelled the witchdoctor to leave the region permanently. The presence of God is invading the territory and driving out the darkness from the spiritual gates and filling the region with light and life. We are well able to take back gradually our communities, cities and even nations for the Kingdom of God.

The kingdom of Heaven has been advancing forcefully, and forceful, faithful believers lay hold of it. "The kingdom of heaven suffers violence, and the violent take it by force" (Matthew 11:12). "May your descendants possess the gates of those who hate them" (Genesis 24:60).

Chapter 10

Can a Nation Be Transformed in a Day?

> Behold, how good and how pleasant it is
> For brethren to dwell together in unity!
> It is like the precious oil upon the head,
> Running down on the beard,
> The beard of Aaron,
> Running down on the edge of his
> garments.
> It is like the dew of Hermon,
> Descending upon the mountains of Zion;
> For there the LORD commanded the
> blessing—
> Life forevermore.
>
> Psalm 133

For 15 years, groups of senior pastors and leaders of churches and ministries in the Greater Colombo Region of Sri Lanka have been coming together to pray for the cities, the region and nation. Approximately 200 evangelical leaders from across all denominational lines meet for prayer and also have an annual retreat and a prayer rally. They come together in unity and pray for the Lord to do a mighty work in the nation.

Psalm 133 has been a key passage guiding and revealing truth about the power of corporate prayer anointing and what could be accomplished regionally and nationally as we engaged in prayer.

> I have set watchmen on your walls, O Jerusalem;
> They shall never hold their peace day or night.
> You who make mention of the LORD, do not keep silent,
> And give Him no rest till He establishes
> And till He makes Jerusalem a praise in the earth.
>
> Isaiah 62:6-7

This Scripture is about the significance of apostolic, intercessory watchmen taking their place over the city and persevering to see profound Kingdom of God advancement taking place.

According to a recent survey, Sri Lanka ranked at 95 in the Corruption Perception Index (CPI) 2016 with 176 countries in the survey.[2] The report released by

[2] http://www.dailymirror.lk/article/Sri-Lanka-becomes-more-

Transparency International, the global movement against corruption, ranks countries according to the perceived level of public sector corruption.

A time of great shaking brought about an unbelievable change!

Who has heard such a thing?

> Who has heard such a thing?
> Who has seen such things?
> Shall the earth be made to give birth in one day?
> *Or* shall a nation be born at once?
>
> Isaiah 66:8

Yes, our nation was reborn on January 8 and 9, 2015! It has been amazing to see the answered prayers. The New Year 2015 turned up with a huge thundering, clashing bang for us here in Sri Lanka. When Melanie and I returned to Sri Lanka on November 22, 2014, we had been in the United States of America and Canada for seven weeks. The incumbent president of Sri Lanka, the Hon. Mahinda Rajapaksa, had called a snap poll for a presidential election. The date was set for January 8, 2015! He chose to call the election early even though he had two years more to complete his second term.

The ruling officials manipulate and change important national events whenever they choose. It is very unpredictable and has the traits of a banana republic, which causes tremendous instability in a nation and is like a roller coaster ride through the political landscape of the nation. The nation under Rajapaksa's

corrupt-122724.html, accessed 1/2/2018.

leadership was heading toward a powerful, totalitarian state with China as its role model and mentor. Sri Lanka, since it was granted its independence in 1948, has been—at least on paper—a democratic nation.

However—surprise, surprise! After announcing the poll date for voting, a senior minister and general secretary of the incumbent president's party without any warning suddenly defected to the opposition side and became the most powerful challenger to the presidency. With the help of a former president and an astute opposition leader, he drew many reputable political parties together to present a huge challenge to the incumbent. The church at large, including our fellowship of churches, called a 33-day prayer watch from December 8, 2014, to January 9, 2015. Hundreds prayed daily for at least an hour for God's chosen person to be appointed. Seventy-two hours of uninterrupted worship and intercession were held from December 31 to January 3, 2015. Powerful! At the conclusion, a 24-hour prayer watch continued on election day, starting January 8 and continuing into the reporting of results on the next day. Thousands joined! Our intercessors had visions of the president's hand turning dark black and withering to the bone. This particular hand had clutched a pure gold amulet that has been chanted over by astrologers and witches for 24/7 protection and success at the polls. He carried his amulet everywhere he went, even on his overseas travels. His personal nationally known "Royal Astrologer" predicted publicly that President Rajapaksa would win easily, as January 8 was a very "lucky day" for him. The astrologer set the date for the elections! This false prophet predicted that it would be far easier than the first and second presidential elections held five and ten years earlier.

Win with between 6.2 and 6.4 votes! The words came into my spirit three weeks before the presidential elections. God had shown me that the challenger would win the election with a total vote between 6.2 and 6.4 million votes. I shared this particular information with some leading national apostolic leaders as we gathered together to pray. When the votes were counted the challenger had obtained 6,217,000 votes. We were shocked at how God had revealed the actual number of votes three weeks before the election. I believe we have entered a time and season when God will give his prophets words and revelations that will amaze the world, once again.

Two days before the election, I [Woody] was called on to pray at a gathering of church leaders convened at a leading senior politician's residence. This man, John Amaratunga, eventually became an important minister in the government's cabinet. Mr. Amaratunga, besides holding other portfolios, is also the Minister for Christian Affairs, which is a department that was so very, very, very needed. For the first time, we have a ministry established by the government, and the grievances for severe persecution that the church has faced over the last 15 years and can hopefully have a voice. Previously, our grievances would go to the Ministry of Religious Affairs under the Ministry of Buddhist Affairs, where it was like going from the frying pan to the fire!

While the votes were being counted, it was during the night that the incumbent, Mr. Rajapaksa, was coming to the realization that he was losing the election. He made a valiant attempt to conduct a military coup so he could remain in power for a third term. At about 2:00 a.m. on January 9, we heard about the attempt and mobilized a group of seasoned intercessors. We pressed through in intercession to stand in the gap to block a military takeover. The military had been dispatched throughout the City of Colombo and other key locations. However, several key players like the army commander, the attorney general, the elections commissioner, and other influential voices just refused to support him. Praise God! The incumbent president finally decided to leave peacefully before daylight and hand over power to the newly elected president. It was like in Bible days when during the midnight hours that Pharaoh was compelled to allow the Children of Israel to leave Egypt after the tenth plague occurred. The shift took place at midnight! Incredible experience in biblical history and now incredible experience during modern-day times.

The atmosphere in the nation has made a huge difference! Astrology and witchcraft were publicly defeated and denounced strongly which was again very unusual. The news outlets reported that the astrologist was wrong, and he immediately left the country fearing for his life. Corruption, nepotism, totalitarianism, human rights abuse, and all the rest have been defeated to some degree, at least for now! The heavy "spell" that hung over the people has been broken. It is like a veil of deception has been pierced by Holy Spirit. People are starting to feel the freedom! Prior to independence in 1948, our nation was under the power of colonialism for centuries.

This time the remnant praying church in Sri Lanka did it right, for which we are very thankful! A sovereign work of God has taken place. The Lord showed me clearly that the current president would be voted in, but that he wouldn't come in without a huge battle. The coup attempt was expected, but the good news is that the remnant, Kingdom-minded Church prayed through and defeated the threat completely! As God's people, we truly are able to take dominion at the gates as the ecclesia, assembly of believers, over the darkness hanging over our nations. We can make a huge difference, if we get involved. If the coup had been successful, the nation could have been under a cruel dictator for many, many years to come. Even though the horse is prepared for battle, victory does come from the Lord! (Proverbs 21:31).

Today, January 19, 2015 Melanie [Woody's wife] and I attended a prayer dedication ceremony at the office of recently appointed government minister Rosy Senanayake, a dedicated Christian. This is historic as she is one of two committed Christians in the new government. This will give the Kingdom of God a higher degree of favor, more than has been known in the history of the nation after independence. Our ministry had been meeting, praying, and counseling with a particular politician for over seven years. Our nation is receiving blessings because of diligent prayer and the gracious hand of our God!

Ask of Me, and I will give You the nations for Your inheritance, and the ends of the earth for Your possession.

Psalm 2:8

We ask for your continued prayer. The official religion in our nation is Buddhism. With a population of 21.6 million, less than 2 percent are evangelical Christians. According to the UK's Open Doors Watch List, which highlights the countries where it is most difficult to live as a Christian, Sri Lanka ranks No. 44, and the source of the persecution is religious nationalism and extremism!

Sri Lanka has never had a revival in its history! Join with us in praying for revival. The time is now!

Revealed in 3/29/16 that President Trump would win!
On March 29, 2016 I was invited by one of our leaders, Brother Jim Hodges, to share a report at a Regional Reformation Institute gathering in Granbury, Texas. As I started to speak, before going to my topic, I declared prophetically that Mr. Trump would win the Republican Presidential Nomination and would go on to win the presidential election on November 2016. That he was the contender who had the capability to defeat the seemingly heavyweight that was challenging him in November. That was seven months before the election, and it seemed to appear that he would not stand a chance to win against the Democratic candidate. But God knew, and his prophets who were pressing in were beginning to hear what was lying ahead.

God is shifting his apostolic leaders to think and hear and proclaim in a new way. We need to rise up to be that breed of seers who can help lead the body of Christ into awakening, reformation and transformation of cities and nations.

Chapter 11

Small Beginnings

Never despise small beginnings.

Zechariah 4:10

Empty handed

In October 1990, I returned to Sri Lanka after my training, learning and transformation from CFNI. I returned empty handed with absolutely zero finances in hand. When I was hired to work as an assistant pastor at a church, my first salary was a mere Rs.250 ($6.00 USD), monthly. I needed about Rs. 15,000 ($365.00 USD) at that time monthly to live a basic human existence. But my heart was filled with such passion and joy to serve God and His people, my meager salary did not bother me at all. My first vehicle was a very small 50cc motor bike. It broke down so much that it was in the repair shop or sitting at home more than it was running.

Big load with no help

As I pioneered a church on the upper floor of a rented house in the Greater Colombo Area, I was doing everything by myself. I swept the 40-seater hall, mopped, set up chairs, furniture and instruments weekly for several years by myself. I did pre-services prayer, led worship and played guitar, took up the offering, testimony time, preaching, did altar ministry, and counselling afterwards and did much, much more. My Sunday was very full from the early days. During the week, I made many house visits, conducted prayer times and a host of diverse activities.

Take time off

From the very beginning I would take an off day on Mondays. That was a good decision to make as many pastors and ministers, especially in my region, were very unwilling to take time off. At first, when you are single and take time off the believers thought Mondays was the best time they could reach me. As I also was living in a room at the rented house for the church people knew how to reach me. When I was firm about time off on Mondays, they were feeling very hurt and rejected. The ones who wanted to meet me on Mondays were the same ones meeting me two to three times a week. After a while, they allowed me to enjoy my off day. It was so important because when I married Melanie five years later, people had already learned to respect our off days. In a culture where people are very communal, they don't understand the boundaries as much. As a result, many pastors and families are weighed down by the burden of the ministry and struggle with marriages, health and with other issues.

Mondays blues

Mondays became miserable days for me sometimes, as I judged success by the number of people that attended the Sunday service and the offerings received. When the attendance was poor, and the church did not grow like I thought it should or have growth like others were, I would be very unhappy. I must have resigned hundreds of times. My precious wife had to put up with my grumbling and griping constantly. She was, however, upbeat and kept on encouraging me numerous times. I am so glad that many years later, God delivered me from measuring success by the number of people attending church. Numbers are needed, but it should not determine the level of joy and sense of fulfillment we were able to have. I recommend that church leaders become free from undervaluing themselves and feeling insecure because of sizes and numbers. It wears pastors down with bitterness, causes negative effects on marriages and families, and attacks the health. Even when we moved into an overseer role as senior pastors/apostolic leaders, we helped our pastoral team to take time off regularly on Monday or some other day. The people were taught to respect their day of rest. It was much easier for them than it was for us as we were there to help them.

Finding a wife

Pioneering and pastoring as a single man has its challenges. You never knew the sincerity of certain young ladies who helped with worship, or worked with the children. Frequently the question was, *What are they really thinking*. They were either sizing me up, or at times I would be left wondering if the young lady was sent by God to become my marriage partner. After several years like this, I was coming to the conclusion that among those I knew, there was no further leading. One Monday night I was so desperate and depressed that I prayed through the entire night, crying out to God to send me a partner of His choice.

Life partner requirements
I had finally concluded that it was possible that God may be sending me a life partner from somewhere overseas. I began to present my conditions to the Lord. The wife should love children, from the U.S, an alumnus from CFNI and ministering in Sri Lanka without any involvement of mine. Missionary dating was out! Actually, that list is like asking for a miracle!

I had met and enjoyed great conversations with Melanie. We met many times when she served at a children's home in Sri Lanka, but then I had reservations thinking how will this American lady settle down to long term serving, and how will I be able support ourselves. She went back to the states, and thereafter I forgot about her. However, after the all-night prayer time I spent time with Jesus about my life partner, the very following Sunday she called me in the middle of the service, "Are you doing ok? I was getting very concerned about you this past week." Right then, I knew she was the person to marry. She called me back later and on September 1, 1995 in Sri Lanka which was August 31, 1995 in Dallas, I proposed to her on the 10,000-mile-long phone call. She said, "Yes!" She only asked, "Do you fix cars?" I replied, "I don't, but I know people who do."

Six months later on March 2, 1996 at the Library Chapel building on CFNI Dallas campus, we married. "Mom" Lindsay attended, Brother Jim Hodges married us, and Dr. Reents gave the homily. Pastor Edgar Terrell and his wife Lillian from Journey Church in Lancaster, Texas, stood in for my parents who were unable to make the long journey from Australia, where they were living at that time.

Humble beginnings

When I brought my bride back to Sri Lanka, our life had humble beginnings. The beginnings were about as humble as they could be, but our love was blind to the challenges. I drove a small, 125cc motorbike, wore orange-colored ponchos to protect ourselves from the rain, and ate Maggi noodles many, many times. Regularly, we had only $4 to pump gasoline. We even had to live in one room at the church for a period of time, because suddenly, the moody house owner wanted us to move out. At Christmas Melanie could only give me five handkerchiefs as a present. I don't think my gift to her would have cost any more than that. But through all the challenges, we were learning to appreciate and love one another. Our beginnings were preparing us to trust God for His leading and provision.

We were learning to enjoy the journey we were on. He who finds a wife finds what is good and receives favor from the Lord (Proverbs 18:22).

Chapter 12

Where His Finger Points, His Hand Supplies

My God shall supply all your needs according to His riches in glory through Christ Jesus.

Philippians 4:19

Miraculous bank deposit

It was time to get a better vehicle. The Nissan B-11 car was old and constantly breaking down. It had been used as much as possible. A Dutch missionary lady was selling her Mazda van and leaving to return home. The van was used but ran well, and cost Rs. 5 lakhs ($5,000 USD). The problem was we only had Rs. 50,000 ($500 USD) in hand. It was early April, and she needed the money at the latest by end of May. She was willing to hand over the van for a 10% down payment and trust our word to have the money in the bank overseas. Fifty days later we could not let her down. God did not let us down!

Fifty days passed quickly, and it was time to bank the money. However, no money came in. Then we received some mysterious but very unbelievably, astounding news. Somebody had anonymously banked Rs. 450,000 ($4,500 USD) in the lady's account at the designated bank in England by May 31, 1999. Until today 18 years later, we still don't know definitely who the donor was. If it wasn't human, it had to be an angel, of course. Praise God!

Because of the blessing of the van, we were able to gift the Nissan B-11 to another pastor who would be able to keep it running. God's economy is quite different than ours!

Every financial giant that was defeated was preparing us in faith and character to face even bigger giants that lay ahead. David had to first defeat the bear, then the lion and ultimately his Goliath. Every enemy he defeated made him stronger for a more fearsome enemy he would face later. The stronger your giant is, the greater your faith will be once your enemy is defeated. Don't shrink back! You are in preparation for greater victories and testimonies.

The unforgettable phone call

Overcomers Church had closed on a deal to purchase our current two-story building for the church on January 8, 2002. It was truly a new beginning. The down payment and the rest of the funds were in the bank but by the deadline, eight months later, September 8, a total of $8,000 was needed to become the owner. No bank or financial institutions would lend the money, even though they would have had the building and property for collateral. Meanwhile, we sensed that the Lord had spoken, "Give 10% from everything we had received." We listened and obeyed by donating to church projects in our region. Our faith was stretched even greater. Over the months, the funds came in various sizes, larger and smaller within the eight months. However, by September 8 we were short of about $8,000 USD (Rs.9 lakhs). That was the final date. We approached the bank manager. Because all the funds had been raised, we begged them for a loan to cover the balance. The bank completely refused!

We returned to our church somewhat shaken and discouraged. But we knelt on our knees to cry out to the Lord. About an hour later, a phone call came from a man in Texas whom we had never met. He asked me how much we were short, then it was like something you would see in a movie. He assured us that he would immediately send the shortfall of $8,000 (Rs.9 lakhs) to us. Phew! That day we saw something shift first in the atmosphere and then in us. Our staff was in shock, but also thankful to the Lord and His faithfulness.

In late 2001, when we were in the U.S., 9/11 had occurred a couple months previously. People were talking about the fact that it was a bad time to try to raise funds. We had to choose to trust God and ignore the naysayers. And then during the 2008 – 2010 recession, we were hearing the same discouraging statements from many people. But every time God honored His promises to us. We don't deny the economic challenges that exist from time to time, but when we choose to place our faith and confidence in the Lord, we lift above the natural into supernatural power to function under spiritual laws that produce success. We cannot and must not let circumstances and man's words limit us or disqualify us. With God nothing is impossible! Every battle that we win is making us stronger for every battle to be faced in the future.

> With men this is impossible, but with God
> all things are possible.
> Matthew 19:26

"Mom" Lindsay

I am very thankful for "Mom" Lindsay who was a wonderful, anointed mentor that showed us how to believe God for supernatural miraculous provision and supply. I listened and watched very carefully how she would encourage people to partner and give. Watching this made me realize several things, and one of the most important was developing relationships. We need people to encourage and support our vision from the Lord, and in turn we encourage and support others for advancing the Kingdom of God. It is like a two-way street. Serving God and serving others. This little grandmotherly-looking lady was a "Super Mom" in the spirit. I had never seen something like this before.

Most students remember her for prayer. She would often say, "When you are here at CFNI, prayer is the most important thing to learn." For those of you who don't know, in 1970 she and her husband Gordon started CFNI with no money, but today it is located on 80 acres 10 minutes south of downtown Dallas and has 43 buildings. I have the highest respect for this amazing woman of God!

Is ministry fundraising still for today?

About ten years back some leaders started teaching that ministry leaders needed to finance their ministry not by ongoing fundraising but by starting side businesses as well. Even we were told, fundraising is not the way to go by several leaders who genuinely were concerned and cared for us. As a result, I tried starting a business or two. But every time I would start a side business, it would fail miserably and even drag me into debt that was very heartbreaking and took several years from which to recover. When ministry or business people would propose that they wanted me to get involved in a business they were doing, I would tell them they would also be in trouble if they chose to do so. Combining business into my already busy life just was not part of my calling from God.

It was like what Peter experienced after the resurrection when he and six others tried fishing. They failed miserably. Some are able to run successful businesses along with their ministries. Not all are called to do so. In my situation, I had been successful in sales as a young man, even winning awards. However, we need to determine what our giftings, strengths and anointing are, and how does God want us to use them. We should continue to function in our giftings and not get distracted or intimidated by others just because it sounds like a good idea. As there is a lot of out of the box thinking in ministry these days and some are revolutionary, we don't have to jump on every band wagon but choose carefully our decisions and choices.

Entering a new era

After the church building, two years later we saw God provide supernaturally to purchase the property for Shepherds Heart Childrens Home. After the purchase of the property, incredibly God provided even more to build the 3-story building for the girls at Shepherds Heart Childrens Home. The fundraising project lasted over two years. And then there were extras that were purchased; things like furniture. At this time, it is a total of 9,500 square feet space. The ministry, property and buildings are truly a sign and a wonder to the community that our God is able to do beyond our expectation. Melanie and I and our leaders stand in awe at what God has done. I had nothing in hand when I started October 1990.

The annual income in Sri Lanka was about $1,400 when we were raising funds. With less than 2% born-again believers, advancing the Gospel has its challenges. Giving and donating to help others, churches and charities is not a common practice in our nation. The Great Commission cannot be limited; therefore, we are extremely grateful for all who have invested in the Gospel. The Great Commission is reaching Sri Lanka!

Chapter 13

Building a Legacy

> The things that you have heard from me, commit these to faithful men who will be able to teach others also.
>
> 2 Timothy 2:2

Aligning with spiritual leaders

In the year 2001 God directed us in a new way to connect and align ourselves with spiritual leaders who had the heart of true fathers and mothers. We needed spiritual alignments that would be new wineskins and provide spiritual covering for us and the vision that God had placed in our hearts, relational accountability not only institutional accountability. New wineskins can receive the fresh revelation and moves of God, while old wineskins are locked into a set pattern of doing ministry.

When we returned to the U.S.A., we sought out spiritual fathers and mothers and made it high priority to spend quality time with them. They were all busy ministers who had good track records in ministering in the U.S.A. and also internationally. It was so empowering to spend time with them and be in their presence. We walked away always feeling empowered, valued and esteemed. When you are properly aligned covenantally, a rich flow of the anointing and authority is imparted. It is difficult for the enemy to take you out of what God has planned. Layers of spiritual protection is invaluable with the various types of assignments you receive from God. You receive greater authority and protection.

Leaders should look for spiritual leaders who will value and esteem you, cheer you on and who will go to war for you. They are the ones that are very important for you to seek out. Someone once said, "Be around leaders who celebrate what God is doing in your life."

It is also important that you be able to have genuine conversations with them not just ones who preach to you the entire time you are with them. They must also be people who are open to the fresh moves of God that occur during these times of reformation and restoration. It is exciting to be around leaders walking in fresh revelation and uphold godly character and integrity. It is important to surround yourself with sound teachers, but also mature, spiritual fathers and mothers who celebrate you and also would speak direction and even correction when you need it. There is an old saying, "Watch out for the three Gs! Girls, glamor and gold!"

Strong prophetic giftings, anointing and mega-influence should have voluntary accountability to maintain integrity. If it's pastoral input or impartation you need, you seek out a leader with a proven, pastoral gift. If it's a teacher, seek out a leader with a proven, solid teaching gift. You need to learn to draw from the multiplicity of gifts available in the body of Christ.

Embracing the next generation

Melanie and I received a prophetic word in 1996 from Barbara Wentroble that really encouraged us and gave us specific direction. She spoke words over me that I did not fully understand at that time, but later changed the way in which we understood and implemented strategies for building and doing ministry. Our theology and philosophy of ministry received a fresh revelation and an upgrade. The prophetic word was also about pouring into and raising up a new generation of younger leaders. "Believe His prophets so shall you prosper" (2 Chronicles 20:20). We received the word, which was about four to five minutes on cassette tape. For several years, we listened to the word as we really sensed the word was from the Lord and bore witness in our spirit. The word was an encouragement, especially when we were discouraged and brought comfort and restoration to us to keep pressing on.

Maintaining consistency

Thereafter, I started taking a few leaders aside weekly to pour into their hearts and equip them. As more continued to join from time to time our leadership team continued to grow and mature. I began with Kumar and his wife Miriam and an evangelistic pastor Sumithra. Later Ronald, Jeremy, Candi, Mich, Herron, Julian, and others were added to this group. In 1996, we started meeting 22 years ago every Thursdays for several hours, and we are still going. Maintaining consistency is very important in raising the generations into leadership and maturity. Inconsistency will not help us accomplish our Kingdom assignments. Like Paul and the early apostles who had a company of ministry leaders around them constantly and was pouring into them consistently.

Home grown
Raising up homegrown talent takes an investment of time. Besides empowerment, we would meet one on one, or later as couples after they were married. We provided nurturing, discipleship and mentoring. Three types of focus to help for healing, growing and maturing. Today the results are starting to come in. They have grown to become our strongest, most reliable leaders who are reproducing spiritual sons and daughters and leading the entire ministry. As the leaders started to develop others, non-home grown spiritual sons and daughters connected and aligned with us as well. In their 30s and 40s now are helping us build a network of likeminded leaders. Our larger vision was to develop and mentor new wineskin apostolic leaders and help them fulfill their calling and God-given destiny. We have poured into them, helped them find resources and saw them go forward in establishing churches and ministries that would be cutting edge in its impact and effectiveness.

At times in the past, we would have selected young potential leaders reside at our house for several years. We would say, "We have to help finish raising you so you can really be godly role models to your generation." Even though at times it was challenging, on the long run it was fully worth the sacrifice and has produced rich fruit. The next generation needs to see us up close and authentic so they know and believe Kingdom values, and daily living of those values is for real life and to be practiced.

Role models

Immorality is a problem throughout society, no matter where we are living and ministering. With modern media, it seems common to observe scandals in churches and ministries. We decided to take a different approach. Our young leaders were passionate about their godly dreams. When we learned, a young man liked a particular young lady, or vice versa, and we were in agreement, we practiced a new approach. As part of the courtship, Melanie and I arranged to have a nice dinner at a restaurant. The young man would propose at the dinner. When our young pastor, Mich, found out what the plan was, he was shocked. Now it has become an interesting pattern and helps young couples to take a mature approach. It is a safeguard against scandals, and it is a new excitement. Not the norm!

Primarily this is for church leadership and not followed in general. Now these leaders are doing the same with their discipled leaders. It is setting a healthy pattern. The young people are attracted to the anticipation of their coming marriage and like the fact that they can proudly talk about their courtship relationship in a positive, healthy way.

This is not the same many times among young leaders in ministry leadership. When Lee Grady, contributing editor for Charisma magazine, ministered in Sri Lanka in 2015, he talked about developing new prototypes for raising up the next generation. Lee commented, "You are building a prototype for ministry and leadership that is unique." Several other well recognized leaders have made the same observations.

Instant obedience

Equipping and mentoring leaders with integrity and character does not come without many heartaches, a great price and sacrifice. One time when Melanie and I were in Dallas, we were busy preparing a newsletter in her mother's apartment. All at once suddenly a strong, overwhelming sense of fear and apprehension gripped me. I heard words whispered in my ear, "The devil is going to try to kill your young leaders back in Sri Lanka. Right now, go into prayer warfare. Don't wait!" It was 12:30 pm in Dallas and would have been midnight in Sri Lanka. We instantly obeyed and prayed for about an hour until we felt the burden and fear leave. About 1:30 pm as soon as we were finished praying, we received a phone call that four of our young leaders had met with a horrible vehicle accident. Our van which they were driving was wrecked beyond repair when they hit a huge water buffalo crossing the road in the middle of the night. The buffalo died on impact, and a neighbor's boundary wall came down, the van was totaled beyond repair, but the four young men escaped with their lives. When the police saw the totaled van, they did not expect that the driver would survive. But he did. Instant obedience by us and the grace of God helped these awesome young men live to go on to destroy the works of the enemy. They are advancing God's kingdom by raising an army of young people across the nation to awaken a generation.

Prayer shield
From the beginning of the ministry, we taught our believers and leaders to put up a prayer shield around their pastors and apostolic leaders. I became aware of this teaching when I studied prayer and intercession under Beth Alves at CFNI. Each day a specific prayer point was to be addressed in prayer for the leader.
1. Sunday: favor with God,
2. Monday: enemies and protection,
3. Tuesday: pure and growing vision,
4. Wednesday: spirit, soul, body and health,
5. Thursday: favor with man,
6. Friday: finances and priorities,
7. Saturday: family.

Dr. Peter Wagner stated that this seven-day, prayer guideline was the best he had seen regarding building a prayer shield around ministry leaders. We followed this guideline carefully for many, many years. At times we felt led to pray a different way on certain days. That is correct, and we need to obey Holy Spirit when He leads a different way. But, in general, we followed this guideline, and it has helped avert attacks and keep layers of protection constantly for the leaders who are on the frontline. I encourage pastors and leaders to put this to use for their leadership and missions teams as it does make a big difference.

Conclusion

A posterity shall serve Him. It will be recounted of the Lord to the next generation.

Psalm 22:30

This book is a testimony to the faithfulness of God and hearing His voice. Every time the testimony is repeated, either by voice or reading. God is glorified!

I encourage each of you, no matter your background, geographic location or age, to become what God has created you to be.

Let God interrupt your life!

Woodrow F. Blok

About the Author

Woody Blok and his wife Melanie have a vision to bring positive transformation throughout the nation of Sri Lanka for over 25 years.

Woody and Melanie are founders and apostolic leaders of Overcomers Church and the ministerial network, Oasis Fellowship, throughout the nation. They also founded and lead:

- Harvest Leadership Institute, accredited with Christ For The Nations Institute in Dallas, Texas.
- Shepherds Heart Childrens Home for abandoned girls, preschool age to 18 years. They reside in a recently built, 3-story home.
- Save Lanka Communities, the humanitarian aid agency, was established in 2001. This NGO is People Touching People caring for hundreds of people during public disasters such as the annual monsoon floods. As well as building water wells in regions where clean drinking water is a tremendous need. During the December Christmas Tsunami 2004, People Touching People reached out to hundreds providing disaster relief.
- Hope Center is a computer training and job creation program for the underserved in the community.

- Woody is a member of the National Prayer Initiative in Sri Lanka and coordinates the longest running pastors' regional prayer network. Meeting monthly for 18 years.

They are both graduates of Christ For The Nations Institute in Dallas, Texas. Woody receive a PhD and Melanie received a Doctor of Ministry from Minnesota Graduate School of Theology in Minneapolis.

Woody has ministered in 12 nations. Woody, Melanie and their daughter Shini live in the Colombo area in Sri Lanka.